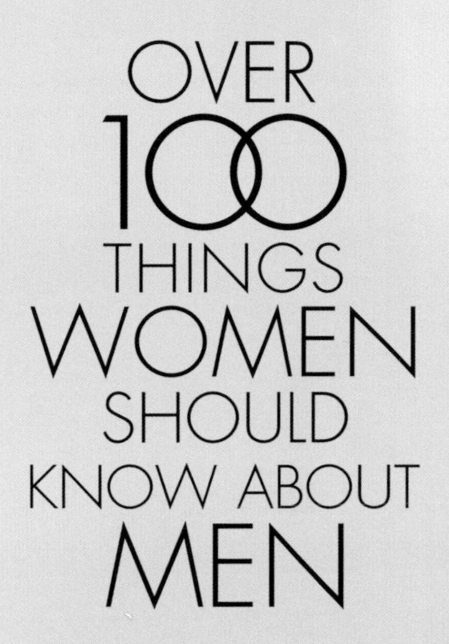
OVER
100
THINGS
WOMEN
SHOULD
KNOW ABOUT
MEN

THIS IS A CARLTON BOOK

This edition published by
Carlton Books Limited 2002
20 Mortimer Street
London W1T 3JW

ISBN 1 84222 451 4

Printed and bound in Singapore

Editorial Manager: Judith More
Art Director: Penny Stock
Executive Editor: Zia Mattocks
Senior Art Editor: Barbara Zuñiga
Design: DW Design
Editor: Toria Leitch
Production Controller: Janette Burgin
Illustrator: Robert Loxton

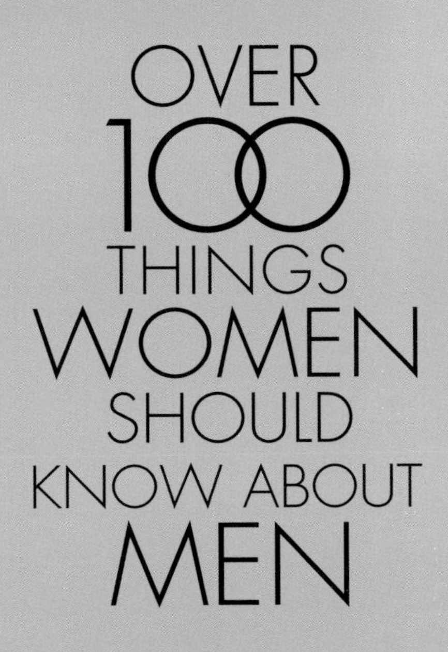

LISA SUSSMAN

his **brain**

If you're anything like the average female, you sometimes have doubts about what planet men come from: Is he for real? Do all guys act this way? What is he THINKING?

Even though men and women both spend nine months in the womb, have 26 vertebrae in our spines and the same neurochemical pathways in our brains, we spend most of our years without any real understanding of what's actually going on in the other's brain.

Well, you can stop head-scratching (and ruining your 'do). Here's your field guide to the male species. This should settle once and for all why someone who pees differently is so different in every other way as well.

Caution: Don't read the following while eating. This unparalleled peek into the male mind may just make your jaw drop.

WHY CAN'T A MAN BE MORE LIKE A WOMAN?

Proof that Mother Nature favours her own sex.

Blahblahblah commitment. Blahblahblah cuddling. Blahblahblah seat up. This is what he hears when you talk. Evolutionary studies have found that the male hearing system isn't as fine-tuned as the female's (something to do with meat hunting being more important than baby nurturing). Hence, cut him some slack when he says he didn't hear you. He probably didn't.

Men and women don't use their brains in the same way. In general, men can only use either their left-brain language skills or their right-brain problem-solving skills, while women can use both at the same time. Which means that if he's talking, he's not thinking and if he's thinking, he's not talking.

From about age 12 to age 30, all men can think about is getting sex. That's because they're biologically driven to spread genes to as many babes as possible to ensure the survival of their DNA. Explaining why men are also so easy.

Why does he leave the toilet seat up, practically guaranteeing you'll find yourself hip-deep in toilet water at 3 am? It's all about power, say psychologists who study this sort of thing. It's his way of saying, `Why is what you want more important than what I want?' (Er, because what a woman wants is more logical, perhaps?)

On the same theme, **his sheets are grimy, not because he has a male 'gross' gene, but because of biology.** Men have a weaker sense of smell and their skin isn't as sensitive as women's. So they aren't likely to notice (until live things are thriving) that they're snoozing on stinky sheets.

The average male is potty-trained by the age of three. So what's with the puddle on the floor? It turns out that peeing straight isn't as easy as it looks. The penis is a dual-purpose machine and many things – including sex – can create a blockage in the pipeline. And drips around the toilet.

It seems he has a scientific excuse for being lousy at figuring out how you feel. A Southern Methodist University found that **men rely on physical sensations, such as a racing heart or clammy hands, to clock moods, while women use visual factors like facial expressions to understand emotions.** Which means that if you're looking for sympathy from him, hand him a stethoscope.

The Y-chromosome set's rabid channel surfing could have something to do with brain degeneration. According to a study conducted at the University of Pennsylvania Medical Center, **men lose brain tissue three times faster than women,** with some of the largest losses in the parts that control attention span (explaining why he doesn't remember your anniversary, even after you've reminded him 623 times).

MEN RULE!

Yes, men need remedial emotional tutoring. But that doesn't mean women still can't learn a few useful lessons about life from them.

He can drive. **In general, men have a better sense of spatial relations and can judge distances better than women.** That's why they tend to do well at things like geometry, figuring out computer games and tail-gating the car in front of them. In other words, he really is more in control than he seems (sometimes, anyway).

9

10

He understands what's restricted information. **Surveys have found that it's WOMEN – not men – who dish the dirt.** He'll never reveal what a great girlfriend he has because deep down he's afraid his friends might go after her (see tip 11). So men stick solely with general reports when with their friends – 'She has brown hair' – whereas women will detail everything down to the freckle on his penis.

11

He knows how to compete – particularly with another man over a woman. Men have a severe need to succeed and, once again, biology is to blame. **In the face of competition, a man's testosterone level soars, making him more willing to take risks.** While this overdrive can be annoying, you may not want to discourage it. According to a study conducted at Pennsylvania State University, testosterone levels of winners stay high post-battle. So if he's lucky, you may get lucky too.

12

The same insensitivity that makes it difficult for him to read people (go back to tip 7) keeps men in good stead for **cutting their losses when a relationship isn't working** rather than making futile attempts to work things out (hmmm – like anyone you know?).

LOSER-PROOF YOUR LIFE

Is he a relationship in the making or the breaking? Checking out his habits is one sure way to know you're not giving your heart to a 'going-nowhere' kind of a guy:

Get down and boogie with him. If he lets you set the groove, you can be sure the same will happen in bed.

Guaranteed orgasms or guaranteed relationship? Five signs he'd be great to Sleep/Live With:

- He never makes you hurry up/He never makes you wait
- He makes big delicious takes-forever-to-clean-up meals/He scrubs all the pans
- He lets you set the pace when you walk/When you start to do something – pour the coffee, pay for the drinks – he often says it's his turn
- Seeing him makes your pulse race/Seeing him puts you in a good mood
- You're on the same wavelength about condoms, where your hot spots are and a threesome with your best friend/You're on the same wavelength about fidelity, commitment and the future

Go shopping with him. Watch how he orders in a restaurant. If he um's and ah's between the red and blue T-shirt or always dithers over this choice of drink, he'll probably buckle under the weight of making any decision – including whether he wants a full-time girlfriend or a casual relationship.

menu

16

Find out how many notches he has on his bed-post. A study in the *Journal of Personality and Social Psychology* states that **the more a guy sleeps around, the more likely his character type falls under the heading 'Creep'.**

Some adult males are men. And some are still men-in-training. Here's how to tell the difference (in other words, he should call you in about ten years):

- He knows what he wants to be doing five years down the road **VS** He's not sure what he'll be doing later tonight
- He claims to be a feminist but still insists on driving, paying for dinner and choosing the contraception **VS** He claims to be a feminist because he says you can drive (translation: he doesn't own a car with a full petrol tank), pay (translation: his credit card is maxed out) and choose the contraception (translation: it doesn't occur to him to ask about it)
- He puts you on the phone when his mother calls **VS** He pretends you're not there when his mother calls
- He starts his own business **VS** He quits his job without having another one lined up

18

BIG FAT LIES ABOUT MEN

You can be so wrong about him.
Here's what he REALLY thinks.

OK, all you cynical, jaded, been-there, done-that, heard-that-line, fell-for-it-anyway, how-could-I-have-been-so-stupid, men-are-the-scum-of-the-earth babes out there. It turns out men aren't the hound dogs we think they are. **When a University of Chicago survey asked men what would make them happy, relationship, marriage and family topped the list while sex came near the bottom.** Maybe that's because marriage is better for him than it is for you – men make more money, live longer, are happier and have healthier, more and better sex when married than women, according to National Health and Social Life survey of 13,000 adults.

19

Men don't fear intimacy with women. What they fear is intimacy with the WRONG woman. **Men, in fact, seek marriage in GREATER numbers than women,** and very few remain lifelong bachelors: 94 per cent of males wed at some point in their lives – and, once a man tries marriage, he's hooked. Divorced and widowed men remarry in greater numbers.

20

Yes, he may be more LIKELY to cheat (see tip 56), but a Gallup Poll has uncovered a virtual epidemic of fidelity: **89 per cent of husbands report the only woman they do the wild thang with is their wife.** As heartening are the results of a Virginia Slims American Women's Opinion Poll in which more than 75 per cent of the 1,000 men surveyed thought fidelity was more important to a good marriage than a satisfying sexual relationship, financial security or having children.

21

You may think that men's body image issues begin and end with penis size. Wrong. The fact is, **94 per cent of men would like to change some aspect of their physical appearance.** And men who think their biceps aren't beefy enough endure the same feelings of inadequacy and depression as women who think their thighs are too thick (see tips 100 and 102 for more on what he fears body-wise).

22

Just because he's throwing darts three minutes after breaking up with you, don't think he isn't hurting inside. Research from the University of Michigan found that **it actually takes men about three times longer to get over a break up than women,** but it usually hits them much later. And they recover by keeping busy (see tip 113 for why). Also, although men don't cry so easily after a break-up, they do get impotent, suffer from gastrointestinal disorders, drink more, have automobile accidents and are more likely to commit suicide over a failed love affair.

23

You are more to him than his career. Asked which factors contribute most to a happy, satisfied life, nearly 2,000 men participating in the Playboy Report on American Men **ranked love second only to health.** Work came an unimpressive fifth. But the way men express their love is by providing for their family (see tip 63 to explain that one).

24

Sure, men would LIKE to have sex seven times in one day – but only once in their lives, so they can talk about it forever. Otherwise, **most are happy to call it a night after one or two body blast-offs** (and fear that YOU aren't – see tip 116).

1-

If one gender had to be labelled starry-eyed romance junkies, it would be the males. **They fall in love faster and more often than females.** Researchers have found that men are more likely than women to fall deeply in love by the fourth date, be the first to utter 'I love you' (once – see tip 51), believe that true love lasts forever and can overcome all obstacles, and are less likely to end the relationship. Awww.

Men are not breast-obsessed. Sure, they like them – a lot. But they don't need triple-letter sizes. When young men were asked to rate front-view line drawings of female physiques for attractiveness in an Archives of Sexual Behavior study, ratings were unaffected by breast size.

Men get soppy. But not over *The English Patient*. Sit with him **when his favourite team loses, however, and you'll see him weep furiously.**

PSYCH HIM OUT

Sneaky tactics guaranteed to make him want what you want – to stay with you.

28

Always be ready to leave. **Men thrive on competition** (reread tip 11) and knowing you aren't totally committed cranks him up a gear into making you want him.

29

If you're looking for a long-term relationship, keep your party dress on until he dials again. Studies show that while the average man will have sex on a first date in a heartbeat, **he doesn't want to get involved with a woman willing to sleep with him on the first date** because he thinks she's doing this with other men (leading to tip 57).

30

Bake him a pumpkin pie. Apparently this scent (along with lavender, black liquorice and doughnuts) spikes penile blood flow, according to a Chicago's Smell & Taste Treatment and Research Foundation study.

Get ahead. According to a University of Utah study, men are 50 per cent more likely to respond to a personal ad where the woman describes herself as ambitious rather than attractive or slim.

Go on The Pill (once you know he's safe). The reality is that he doesn't care about using condoms because he isn't as afraid of AIDS, STDs and pregnancy as you are. And research backs him up. **Women are TWO TIMES more likely to be infected through sex with a man who's infected than a man would be through sleeping with a woman who's infected.**

Say you'd rather stay at home tonight. Researchers at the University of Illinois found that **men are basically nesters,** happiest at home, even while doing the chores. (Women are more likely to go into a joy trance away from la casa.) The reason? He feels more in control in his own surroundings, giving him home court advantage.

Stop dieting. According to University of Texas study, **men love your curves.**

Make it thigh-high and lacy. According to one survey, **lingerie ranked way over toys, games and sharing fantasies as the average male's favourite erotic aid** (by the way, the wowza-wowza combo is high heels and lots of make-up).

his **heart**

As a gender, men have a lot to answer for. Not just warfare, topless models and Arnold Schwarzenegger, but all their pitiable excuses, the total selfishness, the strategic hot-and-cold attitude – all quiet little ways of treating a relationship as anything other than the delicate little soufflé it is.

However, splicing jokes aside, it's clear that the one thing **ALL** men want is a relationship (or at least say they do when you get them alone after a few beers and a particularly bad day). They just don't want to initiate it, work at it, talk about it or think about it. The reality is, men are not trying to avoid **ALL** women – they're trying to avoid all but one. The One.

To understand what makes a man see a woman as the one he wants to marry and other insights into his true desires, read on.

MAN WATCHING

How well do you pick up the silent signals a man sends?

When a guy says he'll call you, it's hard to tell if he means it (see tip 59 for more on this), but **something in the way he moves can provide a few clues:**

- He looks at you: Your bust, that is. And then he makes contact with your eyes
- He ignores you: No guy actively avoids female attention, unless he's already enjoyed yours and decided not to go there again. So this is his pathetic way of trying to make you think he's cool as opposed to desperate
- He stands so close to you that you know what he had for breakfast: He's trying to tell you that he's attracted to you, but in a way that suggests he may be telling you what to wear and who you can hang out with in the future
- He thrusts his chest at you: This is an instinctive move all males make to attract a mate – in short, he wants you

Turn the page for more …

- He grooms himself, patting his hair, adjusting his clothes, tugging his chin: He's saying 'Look at me! Look at me! Look at me!'
- He's rubbing his own arm or chest: He's thinking, 'Me, Tarzan; You, Jane'
- He touches your arm: He feels touchy-feely towards you – get ready for a kiss
- He's sitting with legs wide open: He's an alpha-male, splaying what he's got and saying, 'Come and get it!'

You're clearly giving him the Yes signal but he still doesn't make a move (dammit!). The reason is that he doesn't have a clue. **The way you run your fingers through your hair might mean you want him to kiss you like you've never been kissed before or it might mean your scalp is itchy. Who knows?** He certainly doesn't (see tip 7). So, not to put too fine a point on it, if you want him, take him. He won't mind.

37

38

It turns out that the Crotch Grab isn't just his way of saying, 'Check me out, I'm da man!' **Testicle adjustment is sometimes necessary for the sake of comfort.** These boys get bounced around a lot during the day and need to be put back in place.

ACCESSORIZE!

Girls, it's a jungle out there. He may be tall, cuter than Brad Pitt, hold a job, have ready cash and practically smell of sex, but STILL be a commitment-phobic two-timing jerk. Pay attention to his trimmings – according to psychologists, **things like his favourite colour and snack are what give away his inner bloke.**

39

HE SMELLS OF …

- **Citrus:** Likes hanging with the lads
- **Spice:** Adventure seeker who may suddenly disappear from your life without warning
- **English Leather:** Dependable – he'll always call when he says he will
- **Floral:** He wants to overpower you
- **Musk:** A sensualist. Count on lots of foreplay.
- **No scent:** Macho man. Comes in two types: 1) manly sexist; and 2) grungy slob. You'll smell the difference

40

POSITION YOURSELF IN …

- **Missionary:** A traditionalist
- **Doggy:** He likes submissive women
- **You on top:** He likes a woman who takes control
- **You sitting on his lap:** He stays active while you stay in charge (we'll take him!)

41

HE DRESSES …

- **Bottom Up** (knickers, socks, trousers, shoes, shirt, tie): Well-grounded – he'll always pay the rent and keep his promises
- **Top Down** (shirt, tie, knickers, trousers, socks, shoes): Hates details. Frequently misplaces keys and forgets to call you. But he'll blow his rent money on sexy lingerie for you
- **Varies:** Changeable – might not be dependable

42

HIS SNACK ATTACKS …

- **Crisps:** A social butterfly. Enjoy the ride but You'll need patience (and tips 28–35) to net him
- **Candy:** Still a kid at heart. Sounds like fun … until you have to pay all the bills yet again because he's spent his salary on boy toys
- **Sandwiches:** Tough and determined, he'll work hard to please you
- **Chocolate:** Since choccie contains chemicals that bring on a natural high, his craving for it could signal a need for instant gratification – which won't satisfy your need for commitment

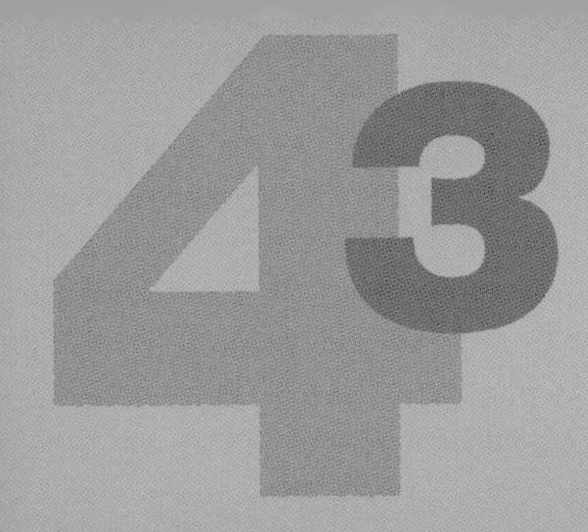

HIS OUTER BEAST …

- **German Shepherd-type Dog:** A crotch sniffer
- **Labrador-type Dog:** Friendly and fun, but needs lots of exercise
- **Corgi-type Dog:** Annoyingly smart but good at respecting space
- **Rottweiler-type Dog:** Protective jealous type – potential abuser
- **Persian Cat:** Hard to please and a bit lazy
- **Short-Haired Cat:** Self-confident
- **Bird/Fish/Any Reptile:** Will back off as soon as it seems you're getting close
- **Rodent:** A secret trainspotter
- **Menagerie:** Easy-going, nurturing and social, but also has lots of demands on his attention

44

Read the sports page for a handle on his nookie stamina. **New studies show that an avid sport fan's testosterone level shoots up 2 per cent after a victory,** leaving him ready for a particularly passionate lovemaking session.Of course, if the team loses, you can always console him with some replay-worthy sex.

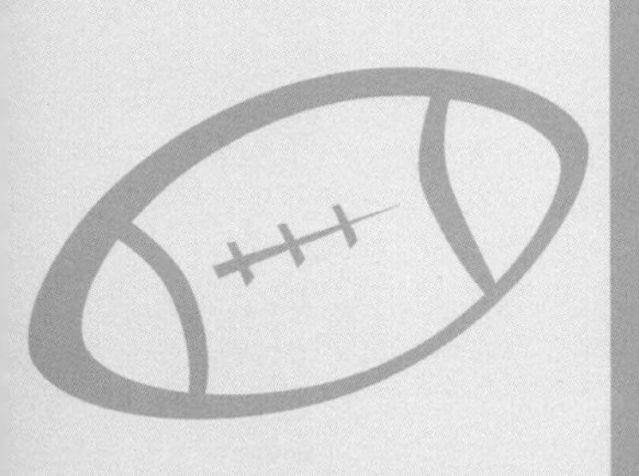

45

Check out his nails. If they're creamy and transparent, he's likely to be a perspirer because the excess moisture changes the nail – which could also mean a nervous personality.

HIS PET GIRLFRIEND PEEVES

Do these and he'll behave like a cornered rat – bolting at the first opportunity.

Talk dirty – about an ex. When you're in love, the desire to open the book to your life is intoxicating. Just remember: men are often insecure sexually (skip on to tip 108) and hearing you've done it all with some other guy can be unsettling. A man's checklist of need-to-know information is short: 'Do you have an STD? Are you on trial for a violent crime? Are you married?' Beyond that, he just doesn't wanna know.

Share too much: He doesn't want you to dish all to your friends, no matter how adorable it was that he cried when his team won the championship. (On the other hand, any tales of his amazing stud abilities are fine for general broadcast.)

Push his head down during sex. He'll get there when he gets there. And he **WILL** get there. Recent polls reveal that muff diving is a top guy activity (right after boning).

Put him through endless chat on the phone. **There's only one type of conversation he gets into – it's called phone sex.**

49

50 ♥

Constantly ask if he loves you. If he's told you once, then that sticks until he makes an exit (see tip 65).

51

Discuss the future. You're together – isn't that enough? Do you have to talk about it all the time? (If you let the 'F' word slip, don't worry – go back to tip 28) .

WHY MEN STAY

What makes a man get down on bended knee.

You're like the girl next door. **Men divide women into two categories – those you screw and those you marry.** He likes wild and crazy – but not to spend the rest of his life with. According to studies, when men are just on the trawl, they seek the Pamela Anderson formula of sexiness. But when they're looking for someone to marry, it's more likely to be someone who is beautiful in their own mind.

52**53**

You caught him at the right 'Tom' moment. There are Toms (as in Cruise) and there are Toms (as in Hanks). One is forever a boy; the other, though boyish, is definitely a man – a man who realizes he wants to marry, have children and settle down. (See tip 17 to decide which yours is).

54

Keep him guessing. **The number one male fantasy is sex with lots of women.** So when you constantly surprise him, he never has a chance to get bored. However, since there are only so many sexual positions, scents, camisoles, lipsticks, breath-freshener tricks and so on in the universe, spread them out over a chunk of time to keep him interested.

55

Making love. Researchers at Bowling Green University found that men rate this one of their top romantic acts, along with giving flowers, kissing, taking a walk and candlelight dinners. The one thing they hardly mentioned? Saying/hearing the phrase, 'I love you'.

HIS CHEATING HEART

What makes a guy roam outside his home turf.

56

A worldwide study of over 37 different cultures established what you knew all along – **men cheat more than women.** The dilemma: they also want to marry a woman with little sexual experience. The reason: they have a biological imperative to spread their own genes but don't want to end up supporting some other bloke's little genes.

57

You suspect yours is not the only station he is servicing. According to research on an average cheat's profile, here's how to know for sure:

- He refuses to consider living together, even though you spend all your time together
- He swept you off your feet (he's a serial romantic)
- He's over-detailed when explaining where he's been/who with and for how long (he's getting his story straight)
- He consistently heads straight for the bathroom before you've even kissed him hello (he's removing evidence)
- He develops an incredible new sexual technique (this one might make it almost worth it)

According to a University of Indiana study, **men are more likely to stray more when:**

- There's a baby in the house (not him)
- Someone else gets ahead of him career-wise (he thinks, 'I'm a loser')
- YOU get ahead of him career-wise (he thinks, 'I'm a wussy loser')
- He has a big win (he thinks he's so cool that everyone loves him and wants him)
- He starts losing his hair – or anything else that reminds him he's getting older, fatter, uglier
- He falls in love (it's his cute way of saying he really cares about you – so much that it scares him right into another woman's arms)
- A woman makes it clear she wants him
- He suspects you're cheating

his **tongue**

There's an old joke about a wife who nags her husband, 'Tell me how you feel'. Finally, the husband blurts, 'I feel … I feel … like watching television'.

The awful truth is, most men have no idea how they feel at any given time. Studies show that men use language to establish difference, separateness and independence (exactly the opposite of women, who talk to connect). So demanding that he talk to you is guaranteed to make him squirm and start rambling about whether new Cheerios really are improved.

Here are the answers and explanations to his biggest verbal 'Huhs?' (you'll be speaking like a native in no time).

59

MAN-SPEAK

An at-a-glance guide to his love talk.

A slew of research has established that men and women use language in different ways. For women, talk is the glue that holds relationships together. To men, conversation is a means, not an end. They don't even like talking to each other that much – two guys can watch a game in silence for four hours and walk away feeling they've bonded. **When men do use words, it's primarily doublespeak to stay on top.** Here's how to make sense of the favourite phrases he uses for different stages of your union:

WHEN YOU'RE DATING

He says: So maybe we could get together or something?
He means: I think you're really hot and want to ask you out, but I'm too chicken to say so

He says: Nothing about seeing you again
He means: His mojo wasn't rising

He says: You're a really good person
He means: You'll never see him again

He says: Let's be friends
He means: You're not my type, but could you set me up with your hot friend?

He says: I'll call you
He means: I really mean to call but I'm scared you'll say Yes, we'll go out and it will be a letdown. Or worse, what if it's not? Do I want to go through all the hassle of dating? Get married? Have kids? Aaahhhh!

He says: We're dating
He means: We've spent at least five nights together, at least one of which has ended in sexual contact. But in no way are we exclusive

He says: We're seeing each other
He means: It's down to you and one other woman

He says: I think we should date exclusively
He means: I'm scared that if I don't make things more permanent, you'll date someone else

WHEN HE WANTS SEX

He says: This is our third date, isn't it?
He says: Is it warm out or just me?
He says: What time do you go to work in the morning?
He says: You think it's true what they say about oysters?
He means: I WANT SEX

He says (in the middle of a great orgasm): I love you
He means: I love that incredible thing you are doing with your finger/tongue/body right now

He says (immediately after making love): It'll be great to show you the house I grew up in (or anything else that smacks of the future)
He means: Are you thinking about your ex and how much better he was than me?

He says: We haven't spoken for ages and I've been thinking about you
He means: I haven't gotten laid in almost three months

He says: I'm not looking to get serious
He means: I just want a little nookie

He says: How many guys have you been with?
He means: I'm the best, right?

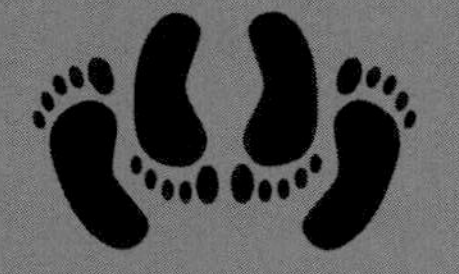

WHEN YOU'RE A COUPLE

He says: I really like you
He means: I think I am falling in love but if I say that word, there is no going back

He says (in middle of a date): It'll be great to show you the house I grew up in (or anything else that smacks of the future)
He means: See above

He says: 'Girlfriend' and he's not doing a Ru Paul imitation
He means: You've made him breakfast, he fixed your car and his buddies aren't allowed to come on to you

He says: Nothing's wrong. I'm fine
He means: God, I know you want to talk about my day and all my interrelationships with my colleagues and boss and the guy who drives my bus, but I am home now and I just want to drink ten beers, eat a bag of chips for dinner and zone out

He says: Maybe we need to slow down
He means: Maybe you need to slow down

He says: I don't know what I want
He means: I don't want you

He says: I need some space
He means: I'm about this close to dumping you but I haven't worked up the nerve yet

He says: You're an amazing woman
He means: You're an amazing woman

He says: I love you
He means: You make me incredible happy whenever we are together. I think you may be **The One**

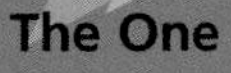

60

As noted in the first tip, **men don't always hear everything you're saying.** Which means he's not always getting your message:

You say (after being introduced): Do you know this band?
He hears: I want you now

You say: What do you do?
He hears: Are you making enough money to make you marriage material?

You say: My ex is a crazy stalker who won't stop calling me. He scares me
He hears: I'm still in love with my ex

You say: What are we doing Saturday night?
He hears: I want all your time for the rest of your life

You say (after making love): That was really nice
He hears: That was the best sex of my life. Let's do it again!

TOP LIES MEN TELL WOMEN

- But I TRIED to call
- I didn't get the message
- I didn't notice what she looked like
- Sex isn't the most important thing
- I'll be careful
- We'll talk about it later
- I'm not mad
- I could fall in love with you in a minute (wait a minute and ask him how he feels now)

TALKING HIS TALK

How to talk to a man so he understands you.

62

Men can only take directions one at a time. So if you want him to go into the kitchen and get you a cup of tea, make it a two-part request (this also applies to when you are in bed with him).

63

When men bother to use words, it's to inspire action (whereas women communicate to bond). So if a guy insults another guy, he automatically thinks he wants to fight. And if you say you like his shirt, he thinks, 'Cool – she wants to jump my bones!'

64

University of Houston psychologists investigating why **men keep things bottled up** found it was to maintain power in a relationship – when they don't talk, their partner is left guessing. You do the same and he'll be putty in your hands (see tip 54 for why).

65

Men don't want to talk about the relationship. They just want to do it (in his mind, if he didn't love you, he'd leave). Here's how he thinks: 'If we need to talk about the relationship, it must be broken. If it's broken, it means it's doomed. I'm outta here.'

66

A man will say, 'I'm fine', even when being tortured by Zulu warriors. **It's in his nature not to reveal weakness because that betrays vulnerability, which comes off as lack of status,** according to research by evolutionary psychologist David Buss. In short, he's worried you'll think he's a weed if he can't solve his problems without his Superwoman girlfriend coming to his aid.

67

There are certain words his tongue seem to trip over – like 'girlfriend', 'love' and 'commitment'. But since men are action-driven (see tip 65), **it's really more important what he does than what he says.** You know your man really loves you if he:

- Lets you drive his car (especially his new SUV)
- Assumes you're spending the weekend together
- Introduces you to his friends
- Stops wearing his 'If you're not wasted, the day is' T-shirt, because he knows you hate it
- Calls for absolutely no reason
- Wants to talk after sex

Here's what he really doesn't want to ever hear from you (and probably won't hear anyway – see tip 1):

- Honey, we have to talk: No, YOU have to talk – and talk and talk and talk
- What are you thinking about?: His feelings, like his answers, will be simple. So if you are lying in post-coital comfort and he answers, 'Pizza', he really means he is thinking about pizza and not that you have skin that resembles pizza or you look like you've eaten one too many pies in your life

- Do you think that girl is pretty?: He thinks that if he even hesitates to say no, it will kill his chances of sex that night – or any other night
- I want to get married: He already assumes this is what you want, he just doesn't want to hear it. So you only have to notify him if this is NOT the case
- How do I look – honestly?: Honestly, you look wonderful to him. That's why he's with you

his **private parts**

SECTION **FOUR**

What's his world view? Depends. Is he: About to have an orgasm? In the midst of having one? Just finished having one?

If it sometimes seems that a man thinks with his penis, it's because he does. Hormones dictate that he has one biological function: to deposit sperm. In anyone, any time, anywhere. In short, the essential distinction between a man and a woman can be summed up in a single word: testosterone.

Now that you understand his primary driving force, it's time to get a handle on that holiest of appliances: his genitals. To be honest, most women don't have a clue as to what's going on down there. You know men pee, zip, tuck, scratch and, every once in a lucky while (they think), they spelunk – and sometimes it seems all at once. But don't worry. There's nothing to programme, no wires to splice. Not a shred of assembly is required.

So roll up your sleeves, and turn down the sheets.

BELOW THE BELT

A do-it-yourselfer's guide to the worldwide family of penis owners.

A man with a big nose just has a big nose. **Actually, the size of his tool depends on his background rather than the size of any other part of his anatomy.** Here's the score, according to a study published by the Charles Darwin Research Institute:

- **Black men:** 16 to 20 cm (6 5/16 to 7 7/8 in) long and 5 cm (2 in) diameter when erect
- **White men:** 14 to 15 cm (5½ to 5⅞ in) long and 3.3 to 4 cm (1 5/16 to 1⅝ in) diameter when erect
- **Asian men:** 10 to 14 cm (4 to 5½ in) long and 3.2 cm (1¼ in) diameter when erect

Get out your stopwatch. Kinsey studies found that **it generally takes a twentysomething three to five minutes to stand to attention** (warning: this reaction time at least doubles with age).

Cool your heels (and other body parts). After orgasm, a man enters a refractory or down period where he has to wait anywhere from five minutes (in his teens) to a day (if he's 50+) until the next stiffy comes along.

Read washing instructions. The following can shrink a relaxed penis by 5 cm (2 in) or more: cold weather, chilly baths or showers, sexual activity, illness, exhaustion, excitement (nonsexual). Seems it's a protective mechanism. **His penis needs a nice warm environment or else it instinctively goes into hiding.**

Three things even he doesn't know about his sperm:

- His sperm has legs. It can live for 5 to 7 days inside you
- It would take a sperm 30 minutes to travel across this page
- A teaspoon of ejaculate can contain more than 600 million sperm (although this is enough to populate the UK ten times over, there's only a 15 per cent chance that one of them will score a direct hit). The average amount of semen per ejaculation increases if he downs a few beers, hasn't had sex since Sylvester Stallone had a hit movie and eats zinc and vitamin C

He may not feel your pain, but he feels another guy's. **The one sure place a man hurts is his groin.** The area is so chockablock full of ultrasensitive nerve endings that they even respond when someone gets a poke in the privates.

75

He gets blue when he doesn't have sex. When a man is aroused, **blood floods not only to the penis but to the entire area.** The longer he stays aroused, the longer the blood stays there. Newer blood is red, but older blood, which has less oxygen, is blue, giving his balls a bluish hue. However, it's not harmful, so don't let him use this as a seduction line.

76

Men as embryos were also women. After testosterone is added, they become boys – but with a few souvenirs left over from his drag queen stint. Such as nipples, a hymen (sitting uselessly near the prostate gland) and a vagina (called vagina masculina, it's a paltry piece of tissue dangling from his bladder). This is all offset by a keen interest in motor sports.

7

HIS BEST FRIEND

His penis made him do it (so don't take it personally).

A recent Kaiser study found that **59 per cent of single men didn't use a condom the last time they had sex.** The top reason: no quickies on the steps (that is, a lack of spontaneity); complaints that wearing a rubber was like eating a steak covered in clingfilm (saranwrap) followed a close second.

If he's a gawker, he may just be following his basic instincts. **Men are programmed to respond to visual stimuli like porn, erotic undies and gorgeous babes in order to spread sperm and propagate the species.** Which is why the quickest way to a man's groin is through his eyes (see tip 87 for how to make him look).

The male member has over 200 different 'official' pet names; the most popular being Mr Happy (he wishes!). Though medical science is still sceptical, men name their penises because they believe the penis has a brain completely separate from their own. How else can they explain why they choose to follow its suggestions on major life choices?

He often has sex with the one he loves. Sex therapists joke that **90 per cent of men masturbate at least once a week and the other 10 per cent are lying about it.** Call it McSex – jerking off is quick, convenient and satisfying without G-spot worries.

DON'T TOUCH

What makes a makes a guy lose his lust.

Common sense tells us that a man may not be erect because he's not excited. But impotence – otherwise known in slang as erectile dysfunction – is often separate from lack of sexual desire. **In fact, in the under-forties set, it is almost always the result of TOO MUCH desire,** which leads to a fear of failure and then to failure itself. (But you knew that already, didn't you?)

No work, no wood. To test the effects of stress on sexual function, researchers had a group of jobless men and a group of employed men watch adult movies. Stress was induced by telling the guys they'd have to talk about their own sexual behaviour and fantasies afterwards to a group of students. When they knew that later they'd have to spill their guts sexually, **the jobless men had poorer erections during the videos than the employed men**. Conclusion: There must be a better way for the unemployed to see free porn.

83

University of Houston studies have found that anger makes his desire wane while anxiety (they used the threat of electric shock!) **actually increases the size of his erections** (stress could make it go either way). Conclusion: Forget about good make-up sex, get him nervous with tip 28 and stop worrying about stressing him out.

Depression is the most common clinical dampener of lust. Even mild levels of the blues can make his noodle droop.

SEXUAL CRAVINGS

No, lots of instant sex with boatloads of women does **NOT** top the list.

85

The turn-on of a woman who gets the sexual ball rolling can hardly be under-estimated (with special bonus points going to those who've tried the greet-him-telling-him-you're-not-wearing-underwear game). Putting his hand somewhere that would get you arrested if you did it in the supermarket goes a long way towards appeasing his secret terror that no matter how deeply attracted he is to you, you won't like him (see tip 103).

86

Because **the penis is where men feel pleasure most intensely,** you can never pay too much attention to it – love it, adore it, worship it. See tips 89–93 for some strategy notes.

87

Because men are much more visual creatures than women (see tip 78), **he doesn't just want to look during sex – he needs to.** If you really want to make his tongue hang out, do it with the lights on.

Similarly, let him see himself naked. Researchers had men sit naked in a chair with and without a board covering their laps. They then watched some porno.

Watching the steamy films, they had the firmest erections when not wearing the board. The point of all this: **Men become more stimulated if they can actually see that they are stimulated.** But don't try this when you are at the cinema.

HOW TO TOUCH A NAKED MAN

Flip his switch and turn him on.

89

Your man has his own G-spot. Owing to its location at the base of the penis, a man's erection is more-or-less anchored upon the prostate, a randy nerve-rich gland so sensitive it even secretes fluid during arousal and ejaculation.
Best Move: Slip a well-lubricated finger through the rectum and probe the rounded back wall of the prostrate. When you feel a firm, round, walnut-size lump, gently caress it while stroking his penis.

A man's erection doesn't end at the base of the penis. There's a railroad junction full of nerves in the perineum, that smooth triangle of flesh between the base of his penis and his anus which, when pressed, will send him straight into an orgasmic swoon.
Best Move: Gently rub the spot with the pad of your finger or thumb. (Pressing really hard with one forceful push can actually stop him from peaking, so be careful.)

90

Stroking his frenulum – the vertical ridge that extends from the tip to the shaft of the penis – will hit his moan zone. Not only are there more nerve endings there, but the skin is also extremely thin.
Best Move: Clenching your pelvic muscles just as he pulls out will give his F-Spot a massage.

Many men are surprised to discover the range and depth of the sensation when you stroke their raphe, the visible line along the centre of the scrotum. They may even end up ejaculating sooner than they (and you) planned.
Best Move: Excite this lust locale by gently running your fingertips along it.

Don't forget his ego – a little stroking goes a long way towards making him relaxed and open to intimacy.
Best Move: Make him feel that you want him (see tip 117).

CAN A MAN EVER HAVE BAD SEX?

Five facts about his Big O – this stuff is so secret even he doesn't know it!

Timing is everything. In short, when he's about to come, let him go with the flow (unless he's aiming for tip 96). If he blows those final few seconds before ejaculation, his orgasm will be a dud, leading to tip 97.

It may seem as though he can have an orgasm just rubbing against a tree. But it's not that simple. **A satisfying experience for a man involves lots of pressure.** That's why the hard thrusting at the end of intercourse is so important. It's what shoves him over the edge (see tips 91 and 92 for how to handle his penis).

95

94

96

He can also have more than one orgasm. In a State University of New York Health Science Center study, men aged 22 to 56 had from three to ten orgasms during extended bouts of sexual stimulation without ejaculation. Their favourite moment: Stopping stimulation just at the brink of orgasm, then starting again once they regained control.

In men, orgasm and ejaculation are not the same thing. The first is the physical and mental release of sexual tension while the second refers to the release of semen, which can sometimes occur without orgasm. In other words, he can fake it too (and 43 per cent have done so at least once).

97

The real reason men snooze after sex: It seems that oxytocin, a hormone that stimulates women's orgasmic contractions and his erection and ejaculation, also causes drowsiness. But because women's bodies normally contain more of it, they may be less sensitive to its surges. Men, on the other hand, fall into a drunken stupor from it.

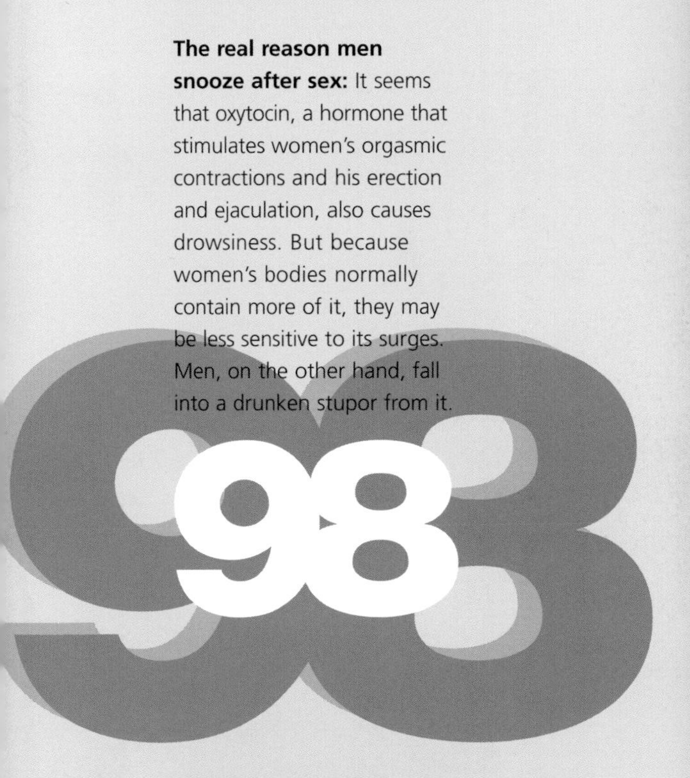

his **hair**

Although men may lead you to believe they can handle absolutely anything, the reality is that your average guy has lots of fears. Even the biggest, strongest he-man can turn into a trembling powder-puff of anxiety given the right circumstances.

And nowhere – nowhere – is a man more likely to have a meltdown than in how he relates to you. Men panic when something threatens their sense of self, and most men's self-concept (as you probably guessed) is rooted in their sex life (read: penis). Put another way, guys freak out over anything and everything from asking you out to making whoopee with you.

Here are the top fears that plague men (not that they'll ever tell you). Use your knowledge wisely.

SECTION **FIVE**

LIFE CONCERNS

Bottom line: Being a man is a scary business.

He's scared of violating the Code of Guys: A man will not appear to be ruled by **his girlfriend, his mother, his boss** or anything other than his penis for fear of being ousted from the group.

He's worried about his thread count: **Most men would rather be castrated than go bald.** The trouble is that everyone can see his hair all the time, while penises manifest themselves only to a chosen few. No one ever had a thinning penis.

He's afraid of you: This can be traced back millions of years to men being awed by things women can do that they can't – menstruate, have children, do more than two things at the same time (if you think men have made any progress after 2.5 million years, try saying tampon in a roomful of guys).

99 100 101

He has height-challenged fears. **More than one in three men report that they'd like to be taller.**

LOVE WORRIES

The more he is into you, the more scared he gets.

His biggest dating doubts:

- **Making the first move:** Because men are often expected to make the first move, we assume they're used to being turned down. Not so. Whether he's 14 or 34, calling you for a date is like phoning the undertaker to arrange his own funeral (see tip 59). Surveys have found that men feel they're putting their manhood on the line every time they ask you out (a little appreciation on your part goes a long way for him)
- **What to talk about:** In his mind, silence equals death. Whenever there's a pause in the conversation he thinks, 'It's over! She's noticed my receding hairline (see tip 100)'
- **Whether to smooch:** Go back to Making The First Move, above
- **Calling you for a second date:** Making a woman wait for the follow-up call is a man's way of gaining back the upper hand. Unfortunately this leaves you in the position of not knowing whether the phone is silent because he doesn't like you, or because he does (see tip 59 for help on whether to call)

He's scared of settling because:

Part One: What if Pamela Anderson calls? No matter how incredible you are (plenty), he's haunted by the possibility of tip 114.

Part Two: He may like you TOO much. Ergo – he wants nothing more to do with you. This is because he either fears a) you won't like him as much; or b) you will, shortly followed by quitting your job, having 16 children, five dogs, demanding a six-bedroom mansion and so on – all of which means he will work for the rest of his life in order to support you.

Part Three: Getting into a committed relationship will tame him. And it will. A Syracuse University study found that testosterone levels are high in single men, decrease in married men and rise in divorced men. This is possibly because single men need to be more aggressive to be able to compete for women, while married men can mellow out because they have the goods and can therefore get on with tip 3.

Part Four: You'll find out that he really does want marriage (although maybe not to you). Go back to tip 18.

Part Five: He will have to start putting the toilet seat down.

He's worried you'll **cheat on him**. Seems it's men who have the real raging hormones. A New Zealand study found that because of his high testosterone levels, he's still prone to jealousy freak-outs and suspicion. So next time he pulls his third degree act, just tell yourself it must be his time of the month.

He's anxious you'll **break up with him**. (see tip 22).

He's terrified **his mother will like you**. Or not like you. Sorry – you can't win this one.

MEET MR SOFTEE

What pushes his sexual panic buttons.

108

Bulletin: **Self-esteem ain't just a girl thing.** Crippling as an unreturned phone call … able to fell tall erections with a single 'It's OK, let's just go to sleep' … devastating as the seventeenth mention of the solicitor-rock-climber-gourmet chef at your gym … in truth, it's amazing he's ever able to perform at all. Bringing us to …

109

He has opening-night jitters. Is it big enough? Will it stay up long enough? **The reality is that men are so often preoccupied with how they'll appear and perform as sexual partners that they're rarely scrutinizing women as much as women fear they're being scrutinized** (in one poll of over 3,000 men, anxiety as to whether he has what it takes to please a woman was the top fear). The possibility that a female he fancies may not want to kiss him, sleep with him, sleep with him a second time or eventually fall in love with him is often enough to make men bail emotionally (explaining why he's uncomfortable and silent the minute after he sleeps with you, even though he is clearly nuts about you – see tip 67 for other ways to tell he's falling hard).

Condoms (see tip 77).

Coming too quickly (causing him to revert to tip 109).

Impotence (see tip 81).

He's worried you'll figure out he doesn't know the way. Men don't ask for directions in bed for the same reason they don't ask for directions in general. Hormones. According to research by evolutionary psychologist Helen Fisher, PhD, communication is linked to the hormone oestrogen. Since men have significantly less oestrogen, they're less verbal and more action-oriented. **That means it's up to you to give your honey a helping hand when it comes to locating your hot spots.**

He thinks he'll never get any again after age 30. According to the University of Chicago's General Social Survey, men have the most sexual intercourse between the ages of 18 and 29. The majority of men in this age-group report bumping bones one or two times a week. After that, the slow, inexorable slide begins. So by age 70, you can expect to be getting lucky only once a month.

He's afraid you'll want to cuddle after sex. Let's face it, **for men, intercourse culminating with orgasm is the main goal.** Everything else is like little paper umbrellas in drinks – fussy and getting in the way of (in this case, his need for – see tip 98) sleep.

115

116 Two words – marathon sex. Guys know women dig tons of foreplay. The problem is, **they confuse body caresses with actual penetration and think you want intercourse to last longer than the re-release of *Apocalypse Now*.** And if they don't go the distance, they fear they'll be labelled a lame lover and you'll therefore seek out a man blessed with more stamina. Result: Every encounter has him straining to break the world record (put his mind and penis at ease by whispering, 'Don't hold back').

117 According to one survey, most men think women are not fond of the penis. Added to this are his insecurities about size and performance (see tip 109). So a woman who lets him know she likes his best friend is the equivalent of a man saying, **'You are the most wonderful woman I have ever met'.**